The Kissing Tree

A Waverley Story Book for Children

Written by Amanda Stanford
Illustrated by Gemma Stuart

The Reworkd Press
Charlotte, 2013

For wee Evie

We see a

beautiful tree.

I kiss you and

you kiss me.

Up, up, up

go the kisses.

Down, down

fall the leaves.

The leaves

drift and blow

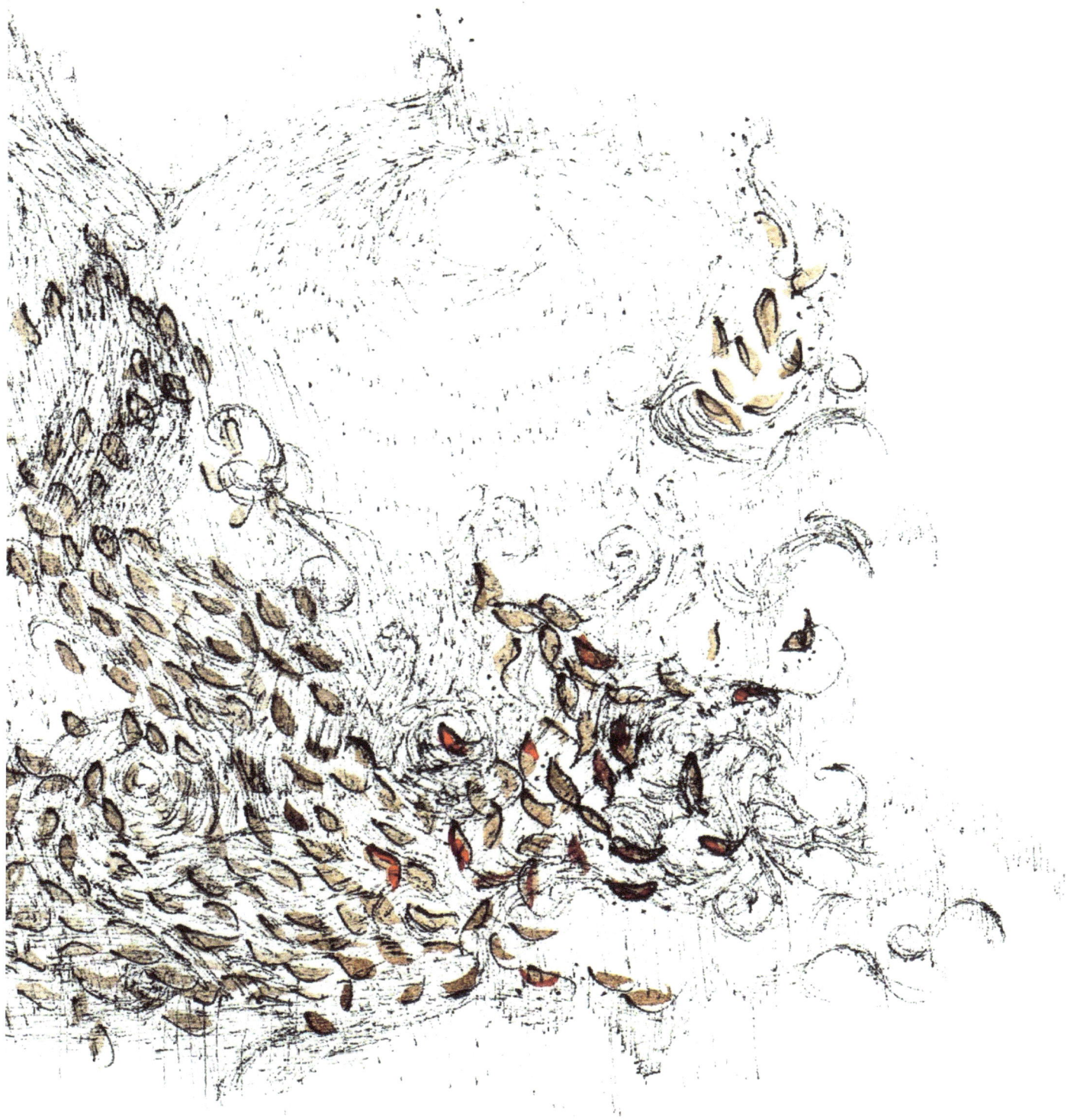

To find the

kissers below.

So when it is we'll remember beneath the

dark and grey,
when we kissed
tree that day.

About the author:

Dr. Amanda Stanford earned her PhD in English Creative Writing from the University of Edinburgh. She has taught writing and English classes for seven years in the US, Mexico, Japan, and Egypt. She also writes historical fiction under the pen name A M Montes de Oca.

About the illustrator:

Gemma Stuart grew up near the sea in Edinburgh, Scotland. She has a degree in Illustration from Edinburgh College of Art and currently enjoys illustrating her own short stories. She participates in several local events, where she sells her art directly to the art-loving public.

www.ingramcontent.com/pod-product-compliance
Lightning Source LLC
Chambersburg PA
CBHW040021050426
42452CB00002B/85